GOD FOR THE REST OF US

STUDY JOURNAL

GOD FOR _____

(INSERT YOUR NAME)

TABLE OF CONTENTS

HAVE YOU EVER TRIED TO EXPLAIN SOMETHING UNEXPLAINABLE?

Maybe you have had to explain what it's like to be in the middle of a tornado to someone who has never been near one. Or what it feels like to fall in love. Or you have tried to describe the color green to someone who has been blind since birth.

SO, HOW DO YOU EXPLAIN GOD'S LOVE?

It isn't easy. The Apostle Paul hints at this in Ephesians 3:17-19 when he writes: "And I pray that you, being rooted and established in love, may have power, together with all the Lord's holy people, to grasp how wide and long and high and deep is the love of Christ, and to know this love that surpasses knowledge—that you may be filled to the measure of all the fullness of God."

Paul says the love of Christ "surpasses knowledge." There just aren't words to describe it. But let's try.

Actually, let's imagine others trying. What words might the people who lived at the time of Jesus, and who watched his life closely, have used to describe his love? How about:

• **Promiscuous?** Promiscuous means to love indiscriminately, to love too many people and the wrong people. Jesus certainly did that. It's what the holier-than-thou-crowd hated about him.

• **Extraneous?** Extraneous means separate from the object to which it is attached. That was one of the other shocking things about Jesus. He loved people who did not deserve it. His love had nothing to do with their behavior.

• **Raucous?** Raucous means to make a disturbance, and Jesus' love did that repeatedly: when he invited himself over to Zacchaeus the corrupt tax collector's house; when he went to a party where sinners gathered; when some guys lowered their friend through a ceiling to get him closer to Jesus' love.

• **Solicitous?** Solicitous means showing interest or concern, being eager to do something. How about the time when Jesus went into Jerusalem, and instead of visiting the holy places there, he went straight to the pool where sick people who needed healing hung out?

• **Vicarious?** Vicarious means acting on behalf of another, and Jesus kept telling people that he had come to represent and share the love of his father in heaven.

• **Infectious?** Infectious means likely to influence others in a rapid manner. We usually think of it as a sick person touching people and infecting them with the disease. Jesus inverted infectious. He was well, touched people with diseases and infected them with his wellness. His loving touch brought healing and transformed the lives of the people who accepted it.

• **Tenacious?** Someone who is tenacious is a person who just won't quit. Think of Jesus fighting against a storm to cross a lake to get to a broken man who lived alone in a graveyard.

• **Efficacious?** Efficacious means effective, and Jesus' love was that. It wasn't just mushy sentiment or something that made people feel nice. When people, like the crazy guy in the graveyard, experienced the love of Jesus, it had an effect. In fact, it radically changed their lives.

• **Courageous?** After all, you could argue that it was Jesus' love and who Jesus loved, that caused his death.

So let me ask you this: Have you truly experienced the promiscuous, extraneous, raucous, solicitous, vicarious, infectious, tenacious, efficacious, courageous love of God? If so, it has turned your life upside down. In fact, if your life is still right side up, I would assume you have not truly experienced it.

One more question: Are you sharing the promiscuous, extraneous, raucous, solicitous, vicarious, infectious, tenacious, efficacious, courageous love of God with others? If so, you're seeing lives turned upside down. If everyone you know still has right-side-up lives, I would assume you probably are not sharing his love.

All of the above are reasons for this study. I pray that this study connects you to the love of Christ, which surpasses knowledge, in a way that transforms you and unleashes you to share it with others. You are going to meet some people from the church I pastor in Las Vegas as they meet Jesus for the first time. Their lives will never be the same. I pray that through this study, your life, and the lives of the people you know, will never be the same.

VINCE ANTONUCCI
God for the Rest of Us author
Verve Church Pastor, Las Vegas

IMAGINE THIS...

You see a well-dressed young couple holding hands walking into a building in front of you. They have two adorable kids who are skipping behind them. How does that make you feel?

Now imagine seeing another well-dressed young couple holding hands walking into a building. They also have two adorable kids in tow. They are a Muslim family and are entering their mosque. How does that make you feel?

Now imagine you're walking behind another couple, also holding hands. This couple is walking into a church, let's say into your church. They are both men. How does that make you feel?

You have three brains.

At least that's a shorthand way to understand what's going on inside your skull, according to some neuroscientists.

For convenience sake, we'll call these three brains the bottom brain, the mid-brain and the top brain.

The bottom brain is at the base of the skull, nearest the spine. The bottom brain controls instinctual behaviors and automatic functions such as breathing and your heart rate.

The mid-brain is called the emotional brain because it's where feelings primarily are processed. The mid-brain can learn, but not think. It acts on conditioned habit more than reasoned thought.

The top brain is called the neo-cortex. This is the grey matter that reasons, plans, discerns and performs abstract thought.

WHAT IS IMPORTANT ABOUT UNDERSTANDING THESE THREE ASPECTS OF YOUR BRAIN?

The premise of this study is that God is for all people, including those who typically are considered "too far gone." God loves the worst sinners as much as the best saints. His love is not based on qualities such as race, gender or age. Neither is his love affected by intentional qualities such as character, fruitfulness or faith. God is love, in and of himself, and therefore his compassion is not altered in any way by the state or actions of its object.

The proclamation that God is for all is the heart of the gospel. If you are a Christ-follower, it's likely that your top brain intellectually accepts these ideas. It can repeat sayings such as:

- "This is love: not that we loved God, but that he loved us and sent his Son as an atoning sacrifice for our sins" (1 John 4:10).
- "He is patient with you, not wanting anyone to perish, but everyone to come to repentance" (2 Peter 3:9).
- "For the Son of Man came to seek and to save the lost" (Luke 19:10).
- "But God demonstrates his own love for us in this: While we were still sinners, Christ died for us" (Romans 5:8).
- "This is love: not that we loved God, but that he loved us and sent his Son as an atoning sacrifice for our sins" (1 John 4:10).
- "Christ Jesus came into the world to save sinners— of whom I am the worst" (1 Timothy 1:15).

However, while your top brain may accept sentiments like these, it is likely that when faced with a real-life deviant—or even someone significantly different from yourself—your mid-brain will react emotionally, and that emotion will carry the day.

So when you read of a corrupt politician being arrested, hear about a mosque going up in your town, or see two men walking hand-in-hand through the mall, what automatically goes through your head? Do you think, "Just like the thief on the cross, Jesus wants to forgive that crooked politician? ... Just like the Canaanite mother, Jesus wants to bless Muslims? ... Just like the adulterous woman, Jesus wants life for that gay couple?"

IF NOT, WHY NOT?

Could it be your mid-brain experiences discomfort or even disgust at some people, then hijacks the rational brain in a rush of fear or loathing? The result is that despite the fact that your thinking brain confesses the Lover of sinners as Lord of your life; your non-thinking mid-brain actually determines how you see and relate to those you find repugnant.

Or maybe it's not just your emotional brain that can't accept Jesus' acceptance of all. It could be your thinking brain doesn't prefer the way of Jesus either. "Whatever Jesus may have said or did, I know God can't really be for the felon, the non-believer or the homosexual. God must be against the meth addict, the exotic dancer, the liberal democrat, the atheistic professor and my ex, who cheated on me—or else God isn't God!"

The message that our heavenly Father is for everyone is a pleasant notion until we run into irritating, unconventional, troubled or cruel people. Then the doctrine is next to impossible to advocate, let alone live out. That's why the purpose of this journal experience is fourfold.

First, to help you become aware of those persons or groups for whom your emotional brain (and maybe your thinking brain, too) says, "Despite what Jesus taught and demonstrated, I am not for them, and I'm not sure God is for them, either."

Second, to help you evangelize this part of your brain— to bring the Good News that God indeed is love—to whatever part of your inner world that doesn't believe God is for even the vilest person.

Third, to help you become aware of any way in which your emotional brain (and maybe your thinking brain) is still saying to yourself, "I know God cannot be for me, because I still am an addict/a skeptic/a struggler/ a failure."

Typically, if you cannot accept that God is for all people, you cannot accept that God is fully for you, either. If God's love is limited by their sin, then His love likely is limited by your sin, too. As you judge others, you subconsciously judge yourself. This self-judgment creates a wall between you and the love of God.

Fourth, to evangelize the part of your brain that still condemns you and has yet to accept God's unconditional, unlimited, unstoppable love for you.

Engaging the whole triune brain, including the emotional brain, takes more than reading Scripture and filling in blanks. Maybe that is why Jesus didn't lead Bible studies or instruct followers to have a daily quiet time. He called people not just to listen to him and discuss his ideas, but to follow him and do what he said. He taught in stories that engage the emotional brain more than the rational brain, then turned his followers into living stories by sending them out on missions and engaging the whole person—head, heart and body.

In a similar way, this journal, while including read and response questions, focuses primarily on practical exercises that can lead to experiences that both reveal and heal.

It will be challenging. You will be prodded again and again to confront the questions:

• Who do I see God being for ... and against? Do I really believe God is for everyone?
• Who am I for ... and against? Who do I view as OK, acceptable, worthwhile, within my circle of love?
• Who do I see as outside, less-than, beyond compassion and within my rights to judge?
• Do I really believe God is for me, even when I'm at my worst?

If you are reading the book *God for the Rest of Us* along with the Small Group Study, here's a guide that will help you know what chapters to read each week.

After Episode	Read Chapters
Episode 1	1, 2, 11
Episode 2	8, 9, 12
Episode 3	3, 4, 5
Episode 4	6, 13, 14
Episode 5	7
Episode 6	10, 15, appendix

>> WEEK ONE

WEEK ONE

This journal involves five morning and five evening times of introspection between each episode. The morning times typically will involve reading and reflecting on scripture, followed by a suggested spiritual exercise for that day. The evening times usually focus on what you experienced or discovered that day from your spiritual exercise.

>> TODAY'S PASSAGE IS JOHN 9.

Before beginning to read, it is important to note that in the Gospel of John, words often hold a double meaning—the obvious meaning and a deeper meaning.

As you read, note in the space below:

- Who is blind
- In what way is the person blind
- What caused the blindness

_____

_____

_____

_____

_____

_____

_____

_____

What do you think Jesus means in v.41? Try to put it in your own words.

_____

_____

_____

_____

_____

Today's exercise is to actively be aware of what you see when other people come into view. When the disciples looked at the blind man, they "saw" a hypothetical question: "Hmmm ... I wonder why he is blind? Did he or his parents sin?" When the religious leaders saw the man, they saw someone "born a total sinner" (v.34 NLT).

When Jesus looked at the man he saw...well, what did he see?

And what do you naturally, automatically see when you look at your spouse, your roommate, your children, your neighbors, your workmates, other commuters or the people on the evening news? Observe yourself observing them, and take note of what you notice. The task is to try NOT to see in any certain way. It is just to notice what you see when you see.

Week 1 / Day 1 / Evening

From those you saw today, choose one person who corresponds to each category below and note what you tend to "see" when you look at that person.

Family member

_____

_____

_____

Workmate

_____

_____

_____

Public figure

_____
_____
_____

Stranger

_____
_____
_____

After today's exercise, what have you observed about
how you see?

_____
_____
_____
_____
_____

What is the Spirit showing you about how you see?

_____
_____
_____
_____
_____
_____
_____

"You say, 'I am rich; I have acquired wealth and do not need a thing.' But you do not realize that you are wretched, pitiful, poor, blind and naked." Revelation 3:17

In 1955, two psychologists, Joseph Luft and Harrington Ingham, created a simple matrix they called the Johari Window. The designation sounds exotic, but it is actually just a combination of their two first names—Joe and Harry. The insightful diagram has been utilized widely. The Johari Window is made up of four main quadrants, those shaded below.

	KNOWN TO SELF	UNKNOWN TO SELF
KNOWN TO OTHERS	**PUBLIC ME** *the me everybody sees*	**BLIND ME** *the me others see, but I don't see*
UNKNOWN TO OTHERS	**CONCEALED ME** *the me I hide from others*	**UNDISCOVERED ME** *the me only God sees*

Each represents a dimension found in every person. The top left room represents the parts of us that are known both to ourselves and to others. This is your public self. Both you and others know certain things about you, such as what you look like, where you work and the opinions you express.

The bottom left room contains what you keep private, that which only you know, but others do not. This is your **concealed** self. It might include things such as private thoughts, secret sins or hidden talents.

The top right area represents those aspects of yourself that others see, but you don't. Others may know that you are beautiful, but you just can't see it. Or they may recognize that you are arrogant, but for you, that doesn't compute. These are your **blind** spots.

The last room is what no one knows about you but God. You may have no idea whether or not you could run a marathon until you train, how you would handle cancer until you're diagnosed or what you would do with five million dollars until you win the lottery. Sometimes we hear people say, "I didn't know I had that in me." Over time we and/or others may discover what is in this room, but for now it is **undiscovered.**

In yesterday's story from John 9, Jesus signaled that the religious leaders had a large blind spot. What would you say kept these experts in sacred law from seeing their self-righteous judgmental behavior and general lack of grace?

_____

_____

_____

_____

_____

_____

What might it take for such a group to see their blindness?

_____

_____

_____

_____

_____

_____

Today's exercise again is about noticing. Keep the Johari Window in mind. Pause occasionally during your day and look at those around you. What do you (and others) see about them that they don't see about themselves? For example: one person may not notice that he has body odor; another may not realize she talks too much; someone else may not see that she has the power to leave her abusive marriage, and her husband may not believe he is an abusive mate. The idea is not to judge others, but just to notice.

Also, ask yourself what is going on that keeps this person from seeing what is obvious to others? Why is this area of life blind to him when it appears so clear?

_____

_____

_____

_____

Week 1 / Day 2 / Evening

Chose three people from your day, and note what appears to be a blind area for each one. Also note what you perceive to be the cause for this blindness.

Person 1:

_____

_____

_____

Person 2:

_____

_____

_____

Person 3:

_____

_____

_____

What came out of this exercise for you today?

_____

_____

_____

_____

_____

_____

_____

_____

What do you find yourself praying for each person?

_____

_____

_____

_____

_____

_____

_____

_____

_____

_____

Read Luke 11:34-36, keeping in mind the last two days of your journal's focus. Then put into your own words what these verses mean to you.

_____

_____

_____

_____

_____

Various translations use different words for the Greek adjective that describes the eye that receives light: good, single, healthy, sound. The better the eye, the more sight and the fewer blind spots. What would you say makes for good eyes that see reality rather than delusion and darkness?

_____

_____

_____

_____

_____

_____

In the Jewish thought of Jesus' day, having an "evil eye" meant one was stingy, hardhearted and closed to the needs of others. Having a good eye meant openness to the lives and needs of others. In Johari Window terms, having a good eye is the way to reduce one's blind area by being open to others and realizing they see things about us that we cannot see ourselves.

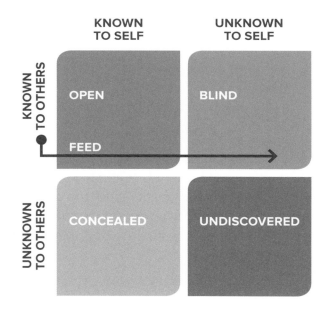

Since the blind area is where others see what we don't see, it is through **feedback** that our eyes open. A person with an "evil eye" will not be open to others' input when it goes counter to his own. He will perceive different viewpoints as a threat, finding reasons to belittle the other and cast them out, as the religious leaders did to the healed man in John 9. However, a person with a good eye will see others viewpoints as potentially valid—even if he can't see their validity at the moment.

Today's exercise is to stay aware of how you tend to respond to information that contradicts your view of yourself or the world around you. For example, if your child pouts, "You never listen to me," is that feedback considered or instantly dismissed? If a coworkers says, "You have great ideas. You should be leading this department," is that feedback weighed or deflected?

As with the last couple of days, don't try to change anything. Just notice what your "eyes" do when information comes your way that doesn't line up with how you already see yourself and your world.

Week 1 / Day 3 / Evening

What did you notice today about how you react to feedback, especially feedback that contrasts with your current view of self and life?

_____

_____

_____

_____

_____

_____

Do you notice a difference between how you react when the feedback is positive and the feedback is negative? Are you more open to positive or negative feedback about yourself?

_____

_____

_____

_____

See if you can come up with a time when you received some kind of positive feedback and your eyes were opened up to a blind spot in your life—to something good that you hadn't seen before. Describe it below.

_____

_____

_____

_____

See if you also can come up with a time when you received negative feedback and your eyes were opened. Describe that experience and its outcome.

_____

_____

_____

_____

_____

_____

Ask the Spirit if there is a blind spot where your eyes need to be opened now. Wait with openness to what might come.

Week 1 / Day 4 / Morning

The pastor we met in the episode, Vince Antonucci, has authored a companion book for this study called, not surprisingly, *God for the Rest of Us*. In Chapter 11, *God for the Pimp*, Vince provides a little more detail about Travis' life.

When Travis got to Vegas, he immediately gravitated to Sin City's nightclubs and strip clubs. Travis had a background in photography and quickly saw his play. He started asking the managers of the clubs, "How about you make me your photographer?"

They laughed and said, "We don't need a photographer."

"Sure you do," he told them, and pretty quickly Travis was the photographer for ten clubs and was employing twelve photographers,

who would take pictures of the party-
ers, sell them as mementos, and feature
them on the nightclubs' websites.

Travis was making good money again, and working
in the nightclub industry meant he was partying and
drinking for free. His dreams had come true, but it still
wasn't enough.

Soon he was recruiting girls to work in the strip clubs.
And he started asking the strippers, "How about you
make me your photographer?"

They'd give him a weird look and say, "But I don't need
a photographer."

"Sure you do," he'd explain, and soon he was
photographing Vegas' strippers.

Then Travis began sleeping with Vegas' strippers.

Since moving to Vegas, Travis' wife had given birth to
their second child. When she found out her husband
was sleeping around, she walked out with the kids.
Travis didn't care. He had other girls now. He could
spend the night with just about anyone he wanted.

And yet it still wasn't enough.

So Travis started hustling the girls. He'd tell them his story and where he was going. And he'd say, "You want to go where I'm going?"

The girls would smile and ask, "For real?"

"Yeah," Travis would tell them. "Only one thing. If we're going to get where we're going, we're going to need some money. You know how to get some money?"

Travis showed the girls how they could make more money with their bodies than they could by just dancing in a strip club. Travis began managing them. Some girls were making him a thousand dollars a night.

Travis' hustle was to make the girls fall in love with him. Then he could get them to do whatever he wanted. He called it his "mind play." And when the occasional girl got fed up with him or tired of living that life, it didn't really matter, because there was always another girl.

One morning when Travis woke up, he looked next to him in bed and saw one of his girls lying there. He walked into the bathroom and looked at himself in the mirror.

Travis had everything he'd ever wanted. He was living the dream.

Here's the question with which we must wrestle: Is God for Travis? Is He for a pimp who sleeps with and sells girls? Is He for this guy who betrayed his wife and left his kids without a father in the house?

How does your thinking brain answer Vince's question?

_____

_____

_____

_____

_____

How about your emotional brain? Is the response different in any way?

_____

_____

_____

_____

_____

Would the response be any different if one of the girls he "sold" was your daughter or granddaughter?

_____

_____

_____

_____

_____

In the same chapter, Vince refers to a famous story found in John 8:2-11. As you read, notice with whom you find yourself identifying in the story.

_____

_____

_____

_____

_____

Those who brought the woman to Jesus for judgment received some "feedback" from him. More accurately, Jesus asked a question that prompted introspection and led to self-feedback. In the Johari Window schema, when insightful feedback is received, the Blind area gets a little smaller and the Open area gets a little larger.

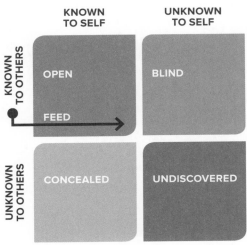

To what were the woman's accusers previously blind but saw more clearly as they walked away?

_____

_____

_____

_____

_____

Here is how Vince follows up the John 8 story:

There was an Old Testament law. The law said that someone guilty of adultery was to be stoned to death.

We learn in this story that, according to Jesus, the only person fit to condemn and punish someone for breaking the law is someone without sin.

That makes sense.

I mean, we don't actually live that way. We condemn people all the time for their sins, despite being guilty of plenty of our own.

We judge the girl who strips off her clothes in the club, despite the fact that we strip people of their dignity when we talk down to them like they're less important than we are.

We condemn the guy who lusts over pornography, despite the fact that we lust after money and popularity.

We disapprove of the unmarried couple living together, despite the face that we live in marriages that doesn't honor God because we don't love one another as Jesus loved the church.

We denounce the girl who wears a low-cut shirt that reveals too much of her body, despite the fact that we gossip and reveal secrets we promised to keep.

We castigate the smoker inhaling nicotine during his work break, despite the fact that we'll inhale three donuts during our work break.

We vilify the man dealing drugs on the street corner, despite the fact that we deal half-truths in business transactions.

I'm not saying that stripping, looking at pornography or living together isn't wrong. It is. It's rebellion against, and violates the nature of, a holy God. It damages the lives of others. If we do it, it demeans us and leads us to live less-than lives. I'm not saying any of it isn't wrong. I'm just saying that we're not in a place to cast stones.

*Well, actually, **I'm** not saying that. Jesus did.*

What's is your reaction to Vince's words?

_____

_____

_____

_____

_____

_____

_____

Feedback from God and others is essential for enlarging one's self-awareness and reducing blind spots. Today, begin a list of people from whom it might be helpful to receive feedback, especially feedback about how you come across to others; how they experience you. As you consider your list, see if you can include a variety of relationship types: family members, friends, workmates, neighbors, etc.

As names come to you today, write them down. At the same time, note what happens inside you when you think of receiving feedback from this person. Does the thought conjure up positive feelings such as excitement or hope, or negative feelings such as anxiety or dread?

(Note: You are not asked to actually seek feedback at this time. That will come later. Just begin your list.)

Name	Initial reaction to the idea of feedback from this person
_____	_____
_____	_____
_____	_____
_____	_____
_____	_____
_____	_____
_____	_____
_____	_____
_____	_____

Week 1 / Day 4 / Evening

Write your honest reaction to the thought of seeking feedback from others about yourself, including feedback about what they perceive to be your blind spots.

_____

_____

_____

_____

_____

_____

Take a few minutes to talk with Jesus about the exercise.
Tell him how you feel, and listen for a response.

_____

_____

_____

_____

Week 1 / Day 5 / Morning

"'What do you want me to do for you?' Jesus asked him.
The blind man said, 'Rabbi, I want to see.'" Mark 10:51

Yesterday you were encouraged to begin a list of people
from whom it might be helpful to receive feedback to
increase self- awareness and reduce blind spots. As you
consider your list, what is your desire level for actually
following through and seeking feedback?

_____

_____

_____

_____

_____

_____

_____

_____

_____

Think of someone you know who appears to be quite open to feedback, who isn't threatened by it and even seeks it out. As you think about this person, what is it inside him that enables such receptivity?

_____

_____

_____

_____

Think of someone you know who appears to be resistant to feedback, even friendly feedback that would be helpful. What is it inside this person that keeps him closed?

_____

_____

_____

_____

_____

_____

_____

Do you want to be more like the open person or the closed person? Explain why.

_____

_____

_____

_____

Vince followed up his teaching on the woman caught in adultery in this way:

Our worth is based on God's love for us. The Bible says in 1 John 3:1, "See what great love the Father has lavished on us, that we should be called children of God! And that is what we are!" We are not defined by our sin but by God's love.

If a person accepted these propositions as true, how would it affect his openness to feedback?

_____

_____

_____

_____

_____

_____

_____

_____

_____

Today's exercise is to write the above paragraph about the basis of our worth. Write it on a card and keep it with you today. When someone says something that stings, feels critical or exposes some blind spot in you, reread those words, and notice the effect.

After completing this day's exercise, think about what has been defining you lately. How well you are doing your job? How well your kids are doing in life? How much or little you are sinning? What friends think about you? How much your Father loves you? Something else?

_____

_____

_____

_____

_____

_____

_____

In his book, Vince described when Travis heard about God's love for the first time.

"Travis started weeping. Uncontrollably. Inconsolably. A few minutes later, just after the service ended, I met Travis for the first time. He walked up to me and tried to speak, but I couldn't understand a word he was saying. He was broken up. Finally, he calmed himself down enough to say, 'I didn't know I could be loved like that.'"

Attempt to sit quietly in the Father's love for you, as if sitting in a pool of light and warmth. Don't try to do anything, be anything or say anything. Just imagine being bathed in compassionate, unconditional concern and interest. Afterward, write your reaction below.

_____

_____

_____

_____

_____

_____

Before your next group gathering, review your work from this week. What stands out to you? What might be helpful to share?

_____

_____

_____

_____

_____

_____

_____

_____

_____

>> WEEK TWO

WEEK TWO

Begin by reading 2 Corinthians 3:2-6, noting what stands out to you.

_____

_____

_____

In the previous episode, Vince quoted unChristian, a research-based book by David Kinnaman of the Barna Group. Surveys showed that young people ages 16-29 had a decidedly negative view of Christians. They sensed words like these:

Anti-homosexual	91%
Judgmental	87%
Hypocritical	85%
Old fashioned	78%

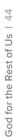

Too political   75%
Out of touch with reality   72%
Insensitive to others   70%
Boring   68%

Kinnaman writes non-Christians "admit that their emotional and intellectual walls go up when they are around Christians, and they reject Jesus because they feel rejected by Christians." In his book The Heart of Christianity (2003), theologian Marcus Borg wrote, "When I ask [my students] to write a short essay on their impression of Christianity, they consistently use five adjectives: Christians are literalistic, anti-intellectual, self-righteous, judgmental and bigoted."

What is your reaction to this feedback?

_____

_____

_____

_____

Which of the descriptive words above do you find to be a common attribute of the professing Christians around you? List those you find common.

_____

_____

_____

_____

What is it about Christians, or maybe non-Christians, that lead to these kinds of survey results?

_____

_____

_____

_____

As you expressed your reaction to the survey results and answered the follow-up questions, how would you describe your "eye?" Would you say you had what Jesus called a "good eye,"—you are open, concerned and willing to consider contradictory input? Or was your eye possibly "bad?" You were closed, dismissive and confident in your own rightness?

_____

_____

_____

_____

When non-Christians receive your "letter" to them (your actions, the way you communicate, etc.), what words would they "read?" Would they be words used above or others? What do you think?

_____

_____

_____

_____

What would you want your letter to actually say? Try writing it out.

_____

_____

_____

_____

_____

_____

_____

Today's exercise is to carry an imaginary letter with you. You may even want to carry an envelope in your pocket as a reminder. As you interact with others, notice the contents of the "letter" you are handing them.

Week 2 / Day 1 / Evening

What did you experience in your exercise today?

_____

_____

_____

_____

_____

Here is some extra credit work. Ask the Spirit to bring to mind one, two or three people. Next, for each he brings to mind, ask him to help you see the letter your typically

write to this person when you encounter him or her.
Then ask him to help you compose the letter he would
like to write through you to each one.

What I usually write   **What the Spirit would write through me**

#1 _____   _____
    _____   _____
    _____   _____
    _____   _____

#2 _____   _____
    _____   _____
    _____   _____
    _____   _____

#3 _____   _____
    _____   _____
    _____   _____
    _____   _____

Week 2 / Day 2 / Morning

The story found in Genesis 3 has been understood in many ways over the centuries. One interpretation suggests that eating from the tree of the knowledge of good and evil represents the beginning of finite human beings usurping the place of God by judging fellow humans. Thus "the Fall" began when man and woman swallowed the lie that they had sufficient omniscience to accurately assess another's true guilt and measure out the just consequences.

Read the narrative with this perspective in mind, and see what you think of this interpretation. Record what strikes you.

_____

_____

_____

_____

_____

Notice the consequences of eating of the tree of good and evil. Immediately Adam and Eve judge themselves, feel shame and hide. When confronted, they blame— another form of judging. Adam blames Eve for giving him the fruit and God for giving him the woman. Eve faults the serpent and apparently implicates God, too, for allowing the creature in Eden. The natural result is alienation. Henceforth the man will be out of sync with the world around him. The physically weaker woman will find herself subject to the stronger male, and the pain in child bearing may point toward the mother trauma of raising children who are constantly arguing and fighting. In the very next generation, this judging spirit devolves into hatred, and a brother (Cain) murders his brother (Abel). The ultimate loss is connection with the tree of life, what Jesus calls "life to the full."

Does this interpretation line up with your experience? When you find yourself assessing and judging others, as if you had sufficient omniscience to know the real truth of what they deserve, what results in you? To put it another way, when you are carrying in your heart a letter of condemnation for others, what are the natural consequences for you, your relationships with others and with God?

_____

_____

_____

_____

_____

Today's exercise is to carry "two letters." The first is a letter of judgment for those you meet. Go ahead and assess their value, their flaws and their performance as if you have the right, all-knowing perspective from

which to do so.

The second letter is the letter of love. This is the letter Jesus gives you to deliver to others, assigning them not the value you see, but the value Jesus conveyed when he died for them.

As you mentally "deliver" the first letter, then the second, notice the effect each has for you.

Week 2 / Day 2 / Evening

Write a reflection on carrying and delivering the two letters, what it was like for you and what you observed.

_____

_____

_____

_____

_____

Walk through Luke 6 with an eye on how judgment factors into this passage. Jot your observations.

_____

_____

_____

_____

How do you find yourself praying in light of today's exercises?

_____

_____

_____

_____

_____

Week 2 / Day 3 / Morning

In the episode, both Warren and Sandra faced difficulty living out their new found faith in their challenging work environments. Vince pointed out that the challenge to be light in the world isn't just for those in crazy Vegas settings, but for all Christ followers in their daily settings. Read the passage to which he referred, Matthew 5:14-16, and the surrounding context of those sayings, then try to describe what you think Jesus meant by saying we are to be light and salt.

_____

_____

_____

_____

_____

_____

_____

Today's exercise is to notice how others recognize you as a Jesus follower. What communicates to others that you are a Christian? Don't try to change anything. Just notice. As you interact with others, ask yourself, "Does this person see me as a Christian? If so, what about me indicates to them that I call Jesus my Lord?"

A second, optional exercise is to keep your eyes open for those outside your usual circles—those who your emotional brain would consider a "them" rather than an "us." It may be those who are different racially, religiously, politically or economically. Over the course of this study, you will be prompted to choose one "outsider" to engage so you can learn what life is like for him and how he sees the world. The idea is not to turn this person into a project, but simply to "discover" him, as we have been discovering the stories of those on the video. For now, the idea is just to be aware of those you tend to see as "other."

Week 2 / Day 3 / Evening

What stands out to you from today's exercises?

_____

_____

_____

_____

Check which of the following you consider to be the most common reasons why others recognize you as a Christian. Feel free to add reasons not listed.

☐ I say I'm a Christian

☐ my generosity with time and money

☐ the joy I exude in tough times

☐ the moral code by which I live

☐ what I put on my social media

☐ religious art or jewelry I display

☐ my service to the needy and hurting

☐ I invite people to church

☐ the people I accept that others reject

☐ the fact I attend church and Bible studies

☐ the warmth they experience from me

☐ the moral stances I take in conversations

☐ how I advertise my business

☐ my positive outlook on life, my hope

_____

_____

_____

_____

Close your evening time by meditating on John 13:35.

Week 2 / Day 4 / Morning

Think of when you submitted yourself to Jesus in a significantly greater way than you ever had before. Write a brief summary of what led up to that greater surrender, and what it was like for you.

_____

_____

_____

_____

_____

_____

_____

_____

_____

_____

What would you say was the most important component or key factor in your decision to submit more of yourself to Jesus?

_____

_____

_____

_____

_____

_____

_____

_____

Look back at the list from yesterday's journal to the reasons people might think you are a Christian. Which, if any, of those factors relate to what motivated you to follow Jesus more closely? For example, was the reason you gave more of your heart to Jesus because he was so moral, or very generous with people, or because he exuded great joy, etc.?

_____

_____

_____

_____

_____

In that time of change, what was your experience of how Jesus looked at you; how he felt about you?

_____

_____

_____

_____

_____

In John's account of Jesus interacting with "the woman at the well," He revealed his intimate knowledge of her. He knew she had five prior husbands and currently was living with a man to whom she wasn't married. He also countered a central tenet of her people's faith: that the proper site for God's temple was in Samaria, not Jerusalem. If you have time to reread the account in chapter four, go ahead and do so. Their conversation ends with the woman going into her town, saying, "He told me everything I ever did. Could this be the messiah?"

In Johari Window terms, Jesus offered this woman feedback that challenged both her Concealed Self and Blind Self. He uncovered her sordid past and contradicted her religious tradition. Yet somehow she considered this good news. What might lead her to think this man, knowing all about her private life and correcting her theology, would be good rather than threatening?

_____

_____

_____

_____

_____

Think of your family and friends. Would you consider it good news if any of them knew everything—absolutely everything—about you? Which one(s)?

_____

_____

_____

_____

_____

_____

_____

Today's exercise again is about noticing. As you encounter others, ask yourself, "If this person knew all about me, what would I anticipate his primary reaction to be? Would it be good news for him to know all about me?"

_____

_____

_____

_____

Write your reaction to today's exercise.

_____

_____

_____

_____

_____

_____

_____

_____

_____

_____

_____

_____

To turn the question around, who among your family and friends would think it good news for you to know all about them? Try to describe why they would or wouldn't think it would be a good thing.

_____
_____
_____
_____
_____

Look back at Jesus' conversation with the woman in John 4. Which of the comments he makes to her are loving for him to say, and which could be taken as cold, judgmental or even obnoxious?

_____
_____
_____
_____
_____

Think about the people from whom you are most open to feedback into your Blind and Concealed areas of the schema. Is there a common denominator among them?

_____
_____
_____
_____
_____

Did your response to the last question have more to do with your "thinking brain" or your "emotional brain?" That is, is your openness to their feedback related to their expertise, knowledge and capability or more to their spirit, heart and feeling?

_____

_____

_____

_____

_____

When people bring us feedback, there are two components: the content of what is said, and the spirit in which it is communicated. Which do you find to be more important when receiving feedback?

_____

_____

_____

As you close your time, reflect on how you experience God's approach to you. When you open yourself to the Spirit in prayer, or read scripture for instruction, what do you perceive to be the predominant emotional mood of God toward you?

_____

_____

_____

_____

When you hear someone say, "I love [insert name], but I don't like him," how does that statement hit you?

_____

_____

_____

What do you think people typically mean when they say, "I love [insert name], but I don't like him?"

_____

_____

_____

Do you find yourself saying, "I love that person, that group, those people, but I don't really like them"? If so, about whom would you say that?

_____

_____

_____

Imagine hearing that statement directed toward you: "I love (your name), but I really don't like him." How does that hit you?

_____

_____

_____

When you hear a statement like that about yourself, do you interpret it as ...

☐ He doesn't like some outward behaviors I exhibit, but he still likes the core of who I am.

☐ He probably doesn't like me all the way down to my core; my essential self.

Today's exercise is to notice what you experience as the primary emotion exuded toward you by those you encounter. What emotion do you feel coming at you?

Do we sense:
- **apathy,** indifference, lack of concern, self-absorption?
- **frustration,** irritation, aggravation, anger?
- **insincerity,** manipulation, smarminess, a user mentality?
- **superiority,** judgment, dismissiveness, condescension?
- **genuine concern,** compassion, enjoyment, delight?

As you consciously experience whatever emotion comes at you, also notice the automatic reaction in yourself.

Week 2 / Day 5 / Evening

What are your thoughts on today's exercise?

_____

_____

_____

_____

_____

Do you have the sense that you usually can or cannot read other people's primary emotion toward you?

_____

_____

_____

_____

_____

Would you say that we usually react to people based on how they make us feel—that is, more out of the emotional brain than the intellectual brain?
Why or why not?

_____

_____

_____

_____

_____

_____

What emotion do you see Jesus presenting in these four passages from Matthew?

- 9:36 _____

_____

- 14:14 _____

_____

- 15:32 _____

_____

- 20:34 _____

_____

From your reading of the gospels, would you say people sensed or experienced this emotion from Jesus when they encountered him? Explain your thinking.

_____
_____
_____

Imagine Jesus looking into your eyes, and saying, "(Your name), I love you, but I don't really like you." Then notice your reaction.

_____
_____
_____

>> **WEEK THREE**

WEEK THREE

"He was despised and rejected by mankind, a man of suffering, and familiar with pain." Isaiah 53:3

In this week's episode, both Scott and Donnie recounted stories of pain and loss. Scott lost his money, his friends, his wife and nearly his life, due to his gambling addiction. We might call his losses self-inflicted. Donnie's losses had more to do with the choices of others and the environment into which he was born. Vince shared some of his story, as well. He spoke of suffering he didn't ask for and from which he still is recovering.

Though their suffering was very different, all three found some measure of redemption for their pain. Recount one story of pain and loss you have

experienced and how it has affected you.

_____

_____

_____

_____

_____

_____

What kind of pain are you in now? What is your current suffering?

_____

_____

_____

_____

_____

Today's task is simply to notice what you do with your pain, past and present, in the various situations you encounter. Is it available for sharing? Is it covered over with smiles and scriptures? Is it tucked away in denial? Are you even aware of it?

Do others know it is there? How do they experience your hurt? Is it used as an excuse or as a lure for pity? Is it an invitation for others to be open, too?

Notice your relationship to your hurts when in relationship to others.

What did you do with your pain when in relationship with others? Was it present and available when connecting with others? Was it walled off and buried? Worn on your sleeve? What are your observations?

_____

_____

_____

_____

_____

_____

_____

_____

What is your sense of Jesus in regard to his pain? Was his pain available to share when connecting with others, or was it more in the background where others wouldn't experience it directly? See if you can support your response with one or more examples from his life.

_____

_____

_____

_____

_____

_____

_____

From your experience with fellow believers, would you say they tend to share their pain or hide it?

_____

_____

_____

_____

Heather Kopp is a longtime Christian author and speaker who is married to a longtime Christian author and speaker. The couple live in Colorado Springs, which is brimming with Christians and is home to the headquarters of multiple Christian ministries. Heather also is an alcoholic who hid her addiction for many years. In her book *Sober Mercies: How Love Caught Up to a Sober Drunk*, she writes about her experience once she came clean and entered recovery:

"The particular brand of love and loyalty that seemed to flow so easily here [in recovery meetings] wasn't like anything I'd ever experienced, inside or outside of church.

"But how could this be? How could a bunch of addicts and alcoholics manage to succeed at creating the kind of intimate fellowship so many of my Christian groups had tried to achieve and failed?

"Many months would pass before I understood that

people bond more deeply over shared brokenness than they do over shared beliefs."

Heather noticed that the above passage is what readers connected with and commented on most. On her blog, she reflected:

"When folks gather around a system of shared beliefs, the price of acceptance in the group is usually agreement, which means the greatest value—stated or not—is being right. Unfortunately, this often creates an atmosphere of fear and performance, which in turn invites *conformity.*

But when people gather around a shared need for healing, the price of acceptance in the group is usually vulnerability, which means the greatest value—stated or not—is being real. This tends to foster a sense of safety and participation, which in turn invites *community.*"*

How do her words strike you?

_____

_____

_____

_____

*http://heatherkopp.com/2014/04/17/the-promise-of-shared-brokenness/

Where have you found the greatest connection in your life?

_____

_____

_____

_____

Week 3 / Day 2 / Morning

Take in the story found in Luke 7:36-50. As you do, note that the description of the woman indicates she lived by prostitution. When it came to women, the term "sinful life" usually meant morally loose. The loose hair indicated a loose life. The perfume would have been a vital asset of her trade.

In v.44, Jesus asked his host, "Do you see this woman?" What do you think he meant by the question?

_____

_____

_____

What did his host *see* when he looked at the woman?

_____

_____

_____

_____

When Jesus looked at her, what did he *see*?

_____

_____

_____

_____

What do you imagine it would have been like to be a prostitute in that day?

_____

_____

_____

_____

What would you guess would lead a woman to sell her body?

_____

_____

_____

_____

Have you gotten to know someone who worked in the sex trade? If so, what did you see?

_____

_____

_____

_____

On Day 5 of last week's journal, you turned to four

passages that described Jesus' emotional response in the face of various people. In each case, Jesus experienced compassion. What must a person *see* to have their compassion stirred?

_____

_____

_____

_____

_____

_____

Yesterday you were asked if you are in pain currently. What percentage of people would you say are in pain currently? _____

Yesterday you also attempted to be aware of your pain while interacting with others. Today, see if you can be aware of theirs. See if you can hear Jesus ask you what he asked his host in v.44: "Do you *see* this woman? This man? This fellow human?"

Then notice what emotion surfaces in you.

_____

_____

_____

_____

_____

_____

What did you *see* today?

_____
_____
_____
_____
_____
_____
_____
_____
_____
_____
_____

What emotions were stirred? Were they different from your typical emotions?

_____
_____
_____
_____
_____
_____
_____
_____
_____
_____
_____
_____

What would a modern-day Pharisee *see* and likely feel, when he looks at ...

	What he *sees*	What he feels
a friend who has left the church		
a Muslim		
lovers living together		
a teen with multiple piercings		
a gay couple		
a crack addict		

What would Jesus *see* and what would he likely feel when he looks at those named above?

_____

_____

_____

_____

_____

When Jesus looks at you, what do you imagine he *sees*? What do you naturally expect he focuses upon? Your sins? Your failures? Your hurts? Your needs? Your heart?

_____

_____

_____

_____

Do you believe that when Jesus looks at you, he is filled with compassion?

_____

_____

If not compassion, then what is he filled with when he looks at you?

_____

_____

_____

_____

"The Lord does not look at the things people look at. People look at the outward appearance, but the Lord looks at the heart." 1 Samuel 16:7

Would it be accurate to apply those words to Jesus?

_____

_____

"Jesus did not look at the things people look at. People looked at the outward appearance, but Jesus looked at the heart."

Why or why not?

_____

_____

_____

_____

For Jesus, what would looking beyond the "outward appearance" mean? What kinds of things did he look past?

_____

_____

_____

_____

_____

When Jesus looked at the heart, what would that include? At what aspects of a person would he be looking?

_____

_____

_____

_____

_____

Since Jesus so often was moved with compassion when encountering people, seeing the heart must have included seeing the heartache. He looked beyond the behavior and saw the underlying hurt. In Johari Window terms, Jesus didn't just see the Public Person— that was obvious for all to see. He looked deeper, into the lower left area of the diagram, to see what was concealed. Could that be why people who triggered disdain in others brought out compassion in Jesus?

_____

_____

_____

_____

_____

_____

_____

In this week's episode, we looked at Donnie, a bouncer in Vegas. How did your feelings about Donnie change as his story unfolded?

_____

_____

_____

_____

_____

Today's exercise is to notice outward appearances that turn you off, whatever they may be. Then ask the Spirit to help you see what might be below the surface—in particular the pain that may be associated with that off-putting appearance.

Week 3 / Day 3 / Evening

What did you notice in today's exercise?

_____

_____

_____

_____

_____

_____

_____

_____

Which of the sentiments below are typically closer to the truth?

Jesus doesn't look at the things I look at.
I usually look at the outward appearance, but Jesus looks at the heart.

I don't look at the things people look at.
People look at the outward appearance, but I seek to see the heart.

If people you know were asked which of these two sentiments best describes you, what do you think would be the general consensus?

_____

_____

_____

_____

_____

Close your time by asking Jesus to show you how he sees.

"So we fix our eyes not on what is seen, but on what is unseen, since what is seen is temporary, but what is unseen is eternal." 2 Corinthians 4:18

Below are two possible ways a person might view Donnie, who was portrayed in the previous episode. What effect would it have on both the person looking and on Donnie?

In each scenario, what might happen to the size and walls of Donnie's Concealed area?

_____

_____

_____

_____

_____

In the next diagram, write what you wish people would look beyond in *your* outward self and see underneath. For example, maybe you wish people would look past your gender and see your intelligence; look past your busyness and see your loneliness, or look past your status as "divorced" and see your daily challenge to keep your head above water.

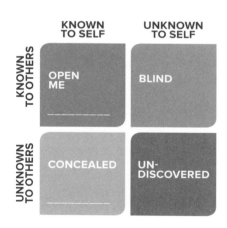

Who sees what you just described?

_____

_____

_____

_____

What is it like for you when someone sees this?

_____

_____

_____

_____

Do you want people to see past your outward self?
Why or why not?

_____

_____

_____

_____

Ephesians 4:2 says, "Be completely humble and gentle;
be patient, bearing with one another in love." Today's
exercise is to continue the practice of humbly looking
beyond the outward appearances of others to see the
underlying story—the heart, the hurts—so you can
approach others in a spirit of gentleness, patience and
compassion.

If you are considering the optional exercise of

approaching someone outside your typical circles to know him better and expand your view, see if you can choose, or even approach, that person today. If you do, approach not to help, but to ask for help. Ask for help in broadening your limited experience, help in understanding a different perspective on the world.

Week 3 / Day 4 / Evening

What thoughts and feelings have you had while practicing today's exercise(s)?

_____

_____

_____

_____

_____

In light of this week's work, what is your reaction to the following assertion?

Transformation is as much about unlearning as it is about learning.

_____

_____

_____

_____

_____

At this point in our study, what would you say Jesus is trying to help you unlearn?

_____

_____

_____

_____

_____

Week 3 / Day 5 / Morning

When it comes to how we see the world, some people tend to sort by similarities, others tend to sort by differences. When sort-by-similarities people encounter others, they notice and focus upon their similarities; what is common to both of them. Sort-by-difference people notice and focus upon the dissimilarities; how the other contrasts with themselves.

As you encounter people today, notice which your automatic brain tends to do: hone in on similarities or on differences.

After noticing your tendency, also become aware of the effect that mode of relating has on you and on the connection between the two of you. Try switching to the other mode and notice the effect.

If you are participating in the optional exercise, notice whether you focus on similarities or differences as you get to know this person outside your usual circle.

Week 3 / Day 5 / Evening

What did you find today? Do you tend to sort more by similarities or differences?

_____

_____

_____

_____

What is your experience when sorting by similarities?

_____

_____

_____

_____

What is your experience when sorting by differences?

_____

_____

_____

_____

Who is easiest to see as someone similar to you?

_____

_____

_____

Who is most difficult to see as someone similar to you?

_____

_____

_____

Would you say Jesus sorted more by similarities or differences?

_____

_____

_____

How does Hebrews 2:14-18 speak to the previous question?

_____

_____

_____

When you think of Jesus, do you tend to focus on your similarities or your differences?

_____

_____

_____

When Jesus looks at you, do you hope he will focus on your similarities or your differences?

_____

_____

_____

Picture Jesus saying to you, "We are very different, you and I." Notice the effect.

_____

_____

_____

Now picture Jesus saying to you, "We are very alike, you and I. You are my brother, my sister." Notice the effect.

_____

_____

_____

Before your gathering, look over your insights from this week. What struck you? What might be meaningful to share with your group?

_____

_____

_____

_____

_____

>> **WEEK FOUR**

WEEK FOUR

In Galatians 5:16-18, we find three different modes out of which a person can be operating at any given time. Read the passage and see if you can spot the three modes.

"But I say, live by the Spirit and you will not carry out the desires of the flesh. For the flesh has desires that are opposed to the Spirit, and the Spirit has desires that are opposed to the flesh, for these are in opposition to each other, so that you cannot do what you want. But if you are led by the Spirit, you are not under the law." (NET)

The first mode is to "live by the Spirit" or be "led by the Spirit." It also is called "walking by the Spirit" or

being "filled with the Spirit." Since we have used the metaphor of seeing throughout this journal, we could say living by the Spirit is like putting on the glasses of Jesus, curing our blindness by seeing as he sees, then responding in his power.

Verses 22-23 describe the "fruit" of living this way. Fruit is not manufactured by a tree, it is the natural outgrowth of a healthy tree rooted in good soil. So the fruit described here is not so much what a person musters up to be a good Christian, but what arises by itself when a person is rooted in the Spirit of Jesus.

As you read those verses, consider times when those qualities flowed naturally out of your heart, as if of themselves. Note some of those occurrences.

_____

_____

_____

_____

_____

_____

_____

_____

_____

_____

_____

_____

What would you say led up to, or brought about, those instances when the fruit of the Spirit sprung up naturally in you?

_____

_____

_____

_____

_____

Today's exercise is just to notice when you feel you are living in the Spirit, walking by the Spirit, being led by the Spirit or wearing the glasses of Jesus—however you choose to identify this way of being in the world.

Week 4 / Day 1 / Evening

What did you observe today about when you were in the Spirit?

_____

_____

_____

_____

When you are in that mode, would you say the fruit arises almost of itself or that you have to manufacture it? What is your experience?

_____

_____

_____

_____

_____

_____

Would you say the mode of being in the Spirit is your usual mode? Why or why not?

_____

_____

_____

When you are in that mode, what do you see when you look at others? List a few family members, friends or even "enemies" who come to mind. Note what you see or how you see them when in the Spirit mode.

Name   What you see when in the Spirit

Add your name to the list above. Note how you see yourself when it that mode. Ask the Spirit how you could stay more in sync with him.

The second mode found in yesterday's passage is called "the flesh." Various ways the flesh mode evidences itself can be found in vv.19-21. What do you think it means to be in the flesh? How does a person operate when they are led by the flesh?

_____

_____

_____

_____

_____

_____

_____

_____

The attributes on the left-hand side on the next page are what is naturally produced when you are in the Spirit. Today's exercise is to consider what's naturally produced in you when you are led by the flesh.

For example, when engrossed by the Spirit, a person tends to love people, care about people and _see_ people. When you are in the mode of your flesh, what do you tend to do in regard to people, how do you tend to relate to people?

Or when in the Spirit, joy tends to flow out, even when

circumstances are difficult. When you are in the flesh, is joy what bubbles up in daily life? If not, what emotion is present instead of joy?

In the **Spirit,** I tend to ...

In the **flesh,** I tend to ...

love, care for, see people

_____ people

know *joy* in difficult times

know _____ in difficult times

feel *peaceful* when under pressure

feel _____ when under pressure

exhibit *patience* with obstacles

exhibit _____ with obstacles

act *kindly* toward the hurting

act _____ toward the hurting

delight in *goodness*

delight in _____

treat the weak with *gentleness*

treat the weak with

_____

be *faithful* in commitments

be _____ in commitments

possess *self-control* with my urges

_____ with my urges

As you engage in your day, be aware of which mode in which you are operating. If and when you find yourself in a fleshlier mode, notice the natural outflow of being that way.

After taking the day to consider it, what would you put in the blanks above? We are not looking for the "correct" responses, but *your responses*—what you actually experience when living out of the flesh. It may help to recall one event during which you know you operated in a flesh-centered mode, then fill in the blanks.

_____

_____

_____

_____

_____

_____

_____

_____

_____

_____

_____

_____

When you are in that mode, what do you see when you look at others? List the same names from yesterday. Note what you see or how you see them when in the flesh mode.

Name   What you see when in the flesh

How do you view yourself when in flesh mode?

_____

_____

_____

_____

_____

How do you tend to see Jesus when in this mode?

_____

_____

_____

_____

_____

_____

How does Jesus see you when you are in the flesh mode?

_____

_____

_____

_____

_____

_____

Would you be open to asking him?

_____

_____

_____

_____

_____

_____

The third mode of being in Galatians 5:16-18 is found in the last line: *"But if you are led by the Spirit, you are not under the law."*

Though Christians are not under the law, they still can live as if they are. That is why Paul so often reminds us of our freedom and warns against returning to a legalistic life. The way of the law is the third way we can approach life.

In summary, we can live in three different modes. Below is a handy comparison of the three and an explanation of each.

SPIRIT	LAW	FLESH
liberty: doing as the Spirit leads	*legalism: doing what the law says*	*license: doing what I want*
rule using	rulemaking	rule breaking
based on faith	based on works	based on works
crucify self	justify self	justify self

Living in the **Flesh** can be described as **license**—doing whatever you want.

Living in the **Law** can be described as **legalism**—doing whatever the rules say.

Living in the **Spirit** can be described as **liberty**—doing whatever the Spirit directs. Galatians 5:1 says, "It is for freedom that Christ has set us free."

The **Flesh** is a **rule-breaking** system. When you are in the Flesh, and you see a rule, you naturally want to break it—step over the line, touch the wet paint, break the speed limit, flaunt authority.

The **Law**, however, is a **rule-making** system. If you notice, those who follow rules are always making more of them. Think of the Pharisees. They knew they weren't supposed to work on the Sabbath, so they made extra rules to make sure they followed that rule: how far they could walk, what was considered work and what wasn't. Think of the church. The Bible says nothing against dancing, smoking or social drinking, but we make extra-biblical rules and expect others to follow them. This is legalism.

The **Spirit** is a **rule-using** system. The directives of God are guidelines, but ultimate obedience is to a Person not a set of rules.

What is the basis of each of these ways of living?

For the **Flesh**, it is **pleasure**. We want what we want, when we want it, to make us feel good.

For the **Law**, it is **works**. The whole basis of the Law is to DO the right things.

For the **Spirit**, it is **faith**. "The righteous will live by faith" which is relationship focused, faith in a Person.

What is the life philosophy of each?

Flesh: gratify self. Do whatever it takes to fulfill self.

Law: justify self. Do whatever it takes to avoid condemnation, receive approval and look good.

Spirit: crucify self. To die to self-effort, self-reliance, self-righteousness and the false self we create apart from God, then live in Christ.

Today's exercise is just to notice when you are living by law, when you are just following the rules for the rules' sake, because you should, to be good and right and are trying to justify and prove yourself. Notice what it is like for you and others. See if you can tell what gets you into the law mode and what gets you out.

Listed again below are the attributes that Paul says are naturally produced when flowing in the Spirit. Think of a time today, or sometime in the past, when you were stuck in law and saw the world through the glasses of rules, ought-tos and shoulds. What naturally grows out of you when in that mode? Do you find yourself loving people? If not, what replaces it? Do you find yourself feeling joyful? If not, how do you feel? Again, we aren't looking for the right answers, but *your answers.*

In the **Spirit,** I tend to ...	In the **flesh,** I tend to ...
love, care for, see people	_____ people
know *joy* in difficult times	know _____ in difficult times
feel *peaceful* when under pressure	feel _____ when under pressure
exhibit *patience* with obstacles	exhibit _____ with obstacles
act *kindly* toward the hurting	act _____ toward the hurting
delight in *goodness*	delight in _____

treat the weak with **gentleness**   treat the weak with

_____

be **faithful** in commitments   be _____
                                    in commitments

possess **self-control**   _____
with my urges   with my urges

When you are in law mode, what do you see when you
look at others? List the same names from yesterday.
Note what you see or how you see them when you are
in this mode.

Name   What you see when in the flesh

How do you view yourself when you are in law mode?

_____

_____

_____

_____

_____

How do you tend to see Jesus when you are in this mode?

_____

_____

_____

_____

_____

In which mode would you say you see yourself and others most accurately, as you and they really are? Try to explain why this mode provides the clearest sight.

_____

_____

_____

_____

How does Jesus see you when you are in law mode?

_____

_____

_____

_____

_____

Would you be open to asking him?

_____

_____

_____

_____

We have been looking at the three modes by which a person can live life. In Galatians 5, Paul set down nine outgrowths of living in Spirit mode. Over the last couple of days, you have considered what natural fruit flows out of you when in flesh and law modes. Below, transcribe what you discovered—the natural fruit that flows from you when in each of the three modes.

When in the SPIRIT	When in the LAW	When in the FLESH
_____	_____	_____
_____	_____	_____
_____	_____	_____
_____	_____	_____
_____	_____	_____
_____	_____	_____
_____	_____	_____
_____	_____	_____

Today's exercise simply is to notice which of these fruits you find to be more of an ongoing state than a temporary experience. What is your "default setting?"

On each of the horizontal lines from this morning, ponder one of the three fruits you tend to gravitate toward. Which of the three is your most common state? For example, on the first line you might have written the following:

When in the SPIRIT

I love people

_____

When in the LAW

I judge people

_____

When in the FLESH

I use people

_____

Many Christians find themselves doing all three at different times. Which do you find yourself doing most of the time—your "default setting?" Circle or check that fruit, then do the same for each horizontal line.

What was this exercise like for you?

_____

_____

_____

_____

What stands out? What do you notice?

_____

_____

_____

_____

Look at your chart when you approach life with Jesus.
What do you notice when doing so?

_____

_____

_____

_____

When you answered the last question, which mode
were you in?

_____

If you looked at your chart while in the mode of the
Spirit, how would you see it?

_____

_____

_____

_____

Week 4 / Day 5 / Morning

Look back at yesterday's chart. On each horizontal line,
in which direction would you say are moving?

_____

_____

_____

For example, on the first line, you might have
circled that you most often are in the flesh, using or
manipulating people. However, you also notice that

though you use people more than you judge or love them, you gradually are using people less and less and slowly loving them more and more. You are moving in the direction of the Spirit.

Or you might have circled that you tend to love people more than judge or use them, but lately find yourself growing in judgment or resentment toward them, and your love is lessening. You are moving toward law. So look at each line, and consider which fruits currently are increasing and which are fading.

_____

_____

_____

_____

_____

_____

Today's exercise is to proactively notice which of the fruits on your chart are increasing, which are decreasing and which way you are moving on each line of the chart.

Week 4 / Day 5 / Evening

What did you notice today? As you consider that question, review yesterday's chart. You might want to mark an up arrow or a down arrow beside each fruit to indicate whether you experience that fruit as increasing or decreasing. You also may want to jot a left arrow or right arrow on each line to indicate which direction you are moving, whether toward the flesh, law or Spirit.

As you look at your chart now, what strikes you?

_____
_____
_____
_____
_____
_____
_____

What do you believe Jesus is saying to you?

_____
_____
_____
_____
_____
_____
_____
_____

Look over your work from this week. What stands out to you? What might be worth sharing with your group?

_____
_____
_____
_____
_____
_____
_____
_____
_____
_____
_____
_____
_____
_____
_____
_____
_____
_____
_____
_____
_____
_____
_____
_____
_____
_____

>> WEEK FIVE

WEEK FIVE

The past episode focused on being willing to jump into the uncomfortable or unknown to take a leap of faith. In last week's journal, we focused on the three modes by which a Christian can walk: the flesh, the law, the Spirit. How might you respond to the challenge to take a risky jump of faith while in each mode? What might your response look like if in the flesh, the law or the Spirit?

**When in the
SPIRIT**

**When in the
LAW**

**When in the
FLESH**

Have you ever taken a leap of faith while in one of the modes? If so, briefly describe it and how it turned out.

_____

_____

_____

The most important leap is from flesh or law to Spirit. If a Christian finds himself in flesh or law mode, how can he make the jump into the way of the Spirit?

_____

_____

_____

A common mistake is to try to be filled with the Spirit by way of the law, to try to do the right things to work one's way into the Spirit. 1 Timothy 1: 8 reads, "We know that the law is good if one uses it properly." We misuse the Law, and so stay under it, and outside the Spirit, in three basic ways:

I. We misuse the law when we try to *prove* ourselves with the law.

Before looking up the verses below, see if you can guess what words go in the blanks.

Galatians 3:10: "For all who _____ on the works of the law are under a _____, as it is written: 'Cursed is everyone who does not continue to do everything written in the Book of the Law.'"

Galatians 5:4: "You who are trying to be justified by the law have been _____ from Christ; you have _____ _____ from grace."

The quotes are from the New International Version, so if you don't use that version, the phrases may not line up exactly. The words that go in the blanks above are *rely, curse, alienated* and *fallen away.* Reread the verses and consider the intensity of the terminology.

II. We misuse the law when we try to *improve* ourselves with the law.

We may think rule keeping will make us better, but it typically makes us bitter. Keeping all the Law is impossible. It feels like an unlimited obligation. Like the Pharisees trying to be perfect, the law can harden our hearts. Following the Law is like reading directions: it may be a good map, but it can't actually take you to the place it describes. It doesn't give you power. It can't be your transportation.

What words would you guess fill in these blanks?

Galatians 3:21: "...For if a law had been given that could impart _____, then righteousness would certainly have come by the law."

Galatians 3:25: "Now that this faith has come, we are no longer under a _____."

The first word is *life*. In Greek, there are two different words for life: *bios* and *zooa*, words from which we get BIOlogy and ZOOlogy. Bios tended to describe physical life, while Zoa tended to describe the higher life, the abundant life. Here the word is Zoa, the law cannot give us the higher, abundant life.

The second word is *supervision*. Other versions variously translate *schoolmaster* (KJV), *guardian* (NLT), *tutor* (NAS). The Greek word is a technical term for a slave who was put in charge of a young nobleman. This slave wasn't his teacher but more his guide or overseer. He made sure he went to school and stayed out of trouble. He was like a babysitter. But when the boy came of age, he no longer had to obey his guardian. The guardian's job was over. So here Paul is saying the law was our overseer, telling us what to do, until Christ came. Now that we have the Spirit, we are under a new Guide. When we use the law to be spiritual, we are going backward, not forward.

III. We misuse law when we *evaluate* others by the Law.

We often love the law because we can use it to categorize everyone else. We can become like corrupt policemen who don't love the law, but instead love the power the law gives them to control or confront others. We can use the law to judge others and justify ourselves. Even when we do succeed, it leads not to praise of God but pride in self. Galatians 5:26, "Let us not become conceited, provoking and envying each other."

Today, notice whether or not you fall into this common trap of trying to take the leap of faith into the Spirit by following the rules, trying harder, being good, trying to attain the Spirit by way of law.

Week 5 / Day 1 / Evening

What did you notice today about how you experienced this morning's assignment?

_____

_____

_____

_____

_____

When you attempt to find life and Spirit by working the law, what results for you? How does that route typically turn out?

_____

_____

_____

_____

Many believers find it seemly instinctive, normal, even automatic to gravitate back to the law—to focus on rules, right and wrong, proving themselves to God and others—to feel like a good Christian. If you notice yourself often falling back under law, what do you sense influences you in that direction?

_____

_____

_____

_____

Would you say Jesus is one of those influences? Does he want you living under the law? Why or why not?

_____

_____

_____

_____

Consider asking him right out, "Lord Jesus, do you want me living under the law?"

Today we will consider more deeply how believers often fall back under the law, and end up less joyful and more judgmental.

Think of when you first encoutered the extravagant grace of Jesus in a profound way—when His unconditional love became real, palpable and experiential. What was that like? What did you receive? Describe it as best you can.

_____

_____

_____

_____

_____

_____

_____

_____

_____

_____

_____

_____

_____

_____

Would the simple drawing on the next page encapsulate your experience?

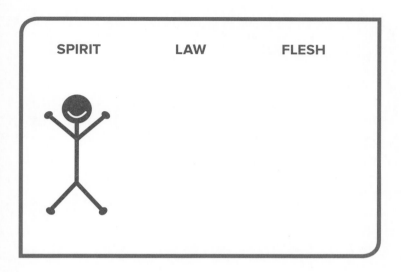

SPIRIT **LAW** **FLESH**

For many, falling under grace is utter joy, total relief, a filling of love for everyone and everything. It is freedom!

If that was the case for you, what happened next in your Christian walk? How would you describe the following weeks, then months?

_____

_____

_____

_____

_____

_____

_____

_____

_____

What came next in your Christian walk when you found yourself living in the Spirit?

_____

_____

_____

_____

_____

_____

_____

_____

_____

_____

_____

_____

For many newly filled believers, they suddenly take their faith seriously. They listen to sermons and ask others for advice on what to do next. They hear things such as, "You should attend church every week" … "have devotions every day" … "attend a Bible study" … "volunteer" … "stamp out worldly activities" … "memorize scripture" … "witness" … "tithe" … always do one thing more.

Gradually, newly filled believers' "faith" becomes a to do list. They slide from the freedom and joy of the Spirit to the endless obligations of the law. More and more expectations are piled on the conscientious Christians until the activities turn into burdens that become heavier and the duties become all-encompassing. See if this diagram resonates with your experience.

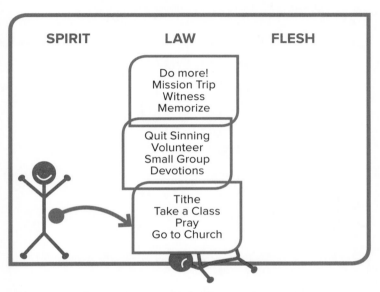

When a person is burdened, exhausted, joy is running out and obligations are piling up, what is the natural reaction? Where do you go when you are stressed, overwhelmed, tired and a little ticked off at all the people who aren't trying as hard as you?

_____

_____

_____

_____

When burdened by the endless law, many will take a leap of faith ... into the flesh for relief. They just want to skip church, veg out, eat a gallon of ice cream, have a few cold beers, go shopping, watch porn, escape to Tahiti—whatever it takes to feel better.

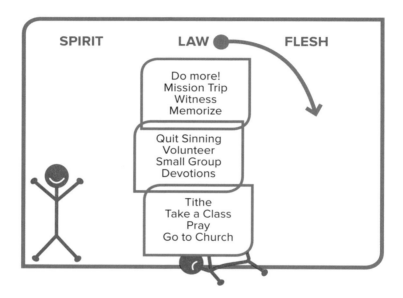

But the flesh disappoints and guilt sets in, so what does the Christian do next? If this is your pattern, what do you do after a stint back in the flesh, gratifying yourself?

_____

_____

_____

_____

Do you find this diagram to be accurate? You rededicate yourself to doing the right things, trying harder, with greater fervor. You return not so much to grace, freedom and the Spirit, but to duty, self-effort and law.

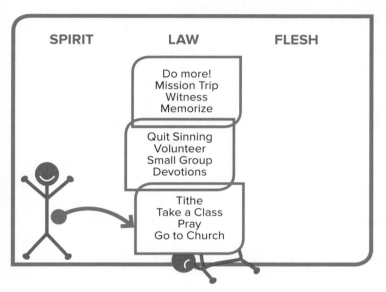

A Christian can end up in an endless cycle of trying to live under the law, burning out, sneaking to the flesh, feeling guilty and rededicating himself to trying harder. Today, keep this pattern in mind. Notice whether you see signs of it in your life, and in the lives of those around you.

If you are attempting the optional experiment of approaching someone "alien" to you, be aware of whether you feel the law pressuring you, and if you retreat to the flesh to escape the pressure.

What did you notice today regarding the cycle described this morning? It may help to plot your day on the chart, noting major activities and in what mode you found yourself during each cycle. You might also note what shifted you from one mode to another.

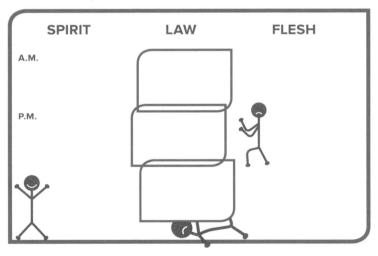

What observations does this exercise bring about for you?

_____

_____

_____

Picture Jesus as you have at other times, full of compassion. What might He see when looking at your day through His eyes?

_____

_____

_____

_____

Week 5 / Day 3 / Morning

We have been considering how we can fall back under law and end up producing the fruit of law, including a self-righteous, judgmental attitude that ends up pushing away people whom Jesus loves. We also have considered how the law can spiral us into the flesh, with its ugly fruit, which often proves to the world that we are not only self-righteous, but self-righteous hypocrites. Then we weighed on how, when we try to right ourselves, we can fall into the trap of attempting to use the law to become re-inspired with the Spirit. But as we saw on Day 1, the law cannot give us life. According to Galatians 3:24, what was the purpose of the law?

> *"So the law was our guardian until Christ came that we might be justified by faith."*

The law is supposed to drive us to give up our attempts

to justify and perfect ourselves through self effort and to surrender to faith. The law is given not as a stairway to the Spirit but as a wall that reveals our need for the Spirit. If a person finds himself in the flesh or law, how does he find his way back into the Spirit? Chew on Galatians 3:1-5, with the commentary in parentheses.

> *You foolish Galatians! (Fool is a strong word. Proverbs says, "The fool says in his heart there is no God.")*
>
> *Who has bewitched you? (Cast a spell over you, because what you are doing is crazy!)*
>
> *Before your very eyes Jesus Christ was clearly portrayed as crucified. (Paul's original message to them was so powerful, that it is was obvious to all what Jesus had done for them.)*
>
> *I would like to learn just one thing from you: Did you receive the Spirit by the works of the law, or by believing what you heard? (How would you answer that question for yourself?)*
>
> *Are you so foolish? (There's that strong word again.)*
>
> *After beginning by means of the Spirit, are you*

now trying to finish (perfect yourself, complete your mission) by means of the flesh (by your own ability, work, strength)?

Have you experienced so much in vain—if it really was in vain? (The results of your efforts apart from the Spirit: nothing. As Jesus said, "Apart from me, you can do nothing." (John 15:5)).

" ... Does God give you his Spirit and work miracles among you by the works of the law, or by your believing what you heard?" (And the answer is ... ?)

Could it be that the way to live in the Spirit, or return to the Spirit when we have lost our way, is to by taking the same path by which we received the Spirit initially: by faith, by trusting in the incredible, unstoppable, all-sufficient love and grace of God through Christ? As Travis said in Episode 1, "To think that God could love someone like me has really changed my life."

The same way we got in is the way we stay in. The Spirit was a gift from the start: Review Acts 2:38:

"Peter replied, 'Repent and be baptized, every one of you, in the name of Jesus Christ for the forgiveness of your sins. And you will receive the gift of the Holy Spirit.'"

We cannot earn the Spirit through good deeds. The Spirit is a gift we receive by trusting in God's utter goodness. In the law and the flesh, there also is the element of trust. Today try to discern what you are trusting in when you find yourself in each mode. When you detect you are in a fleshy mode, ask yourself what you are putting your faith in at that point. When you find yourself in a legalistic frame, ask yourself what you are trusting then. When you become aware you are experiencing the Spirit, check where your faith is placed, as well.

Week 5 / Day 3 / Evening

It was suggested this morning that faith is involved in each operating mode. When you are in flesh mode, in whom or what do you tend to put your faith? With what is that going to fill you, "save" you and make life OK? Write it in the box on the next page.

When you are in law mode, trying to do all the right things, where is your faith placed? Who or what is going to make all the good deeds happen so you can feel good about yourself and justified before God and others?

When you have experienced the freedom and life of the Spirit, where was your trust placed? How would you describe it?

In prior diagrams, a stick figure was pictured under each mode. In this one, draw your own figure, representing your experience while in that mode. What do you tend to look like when living in the flesh, the law and the Spirit, trusting the things you trust in each?

SPIRIT	**LAW**	**FLESH**
Faith in...	*Faith in...*	*Faith in...*

What is your reaction to today's work?

_____

_____

_____

_____

_____

_____

_____

_____

"So from now on we regard no one from a worldly point of view. Though we once regarded Christ in this way, we do so no longer." 2 Corinthians 5:16

The direction of this study has been to confront us with questions such as: Do I think God actually loves everyone? Do I believe He is seeking everyone, wants everyone, desires the best for everyone? Is God really for those on the fringes who have been cast aside, considered too far gone, written off, even despised and hated? Is God actually for … ALL … no matter what?

Who am I for, and who am I actually against, in my emotional brain and in my rational brain?

Over the last two weeks, this journal has focused on three modes in which a Christian can answer the questions above. Today, notice afresh how you see the people around you while in each mode. In a sense, carry three sets of glasses with you today: the spectacles of the flesh, the law and the Spirit. As you observe or converse with others, imagine yourself looking through each pair of lenses. What do you notice when wearing each? What do you see? How do you see?

You may want to spend a few minutes "practicing" this

morning, prayerfully picturing different people and
noting what you "see."

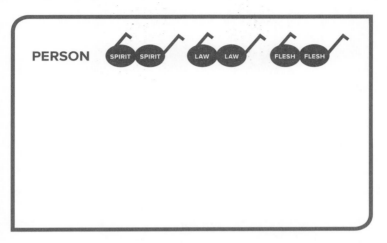

Week 5 / Day 4 / Morning

In this morning's diagram, jot some of the things you
saw in others today while wearing each pair of glasses.

_____
_____
_____
_____
_____
_____
_____
_____

Wearing which glasses afforded you the most accurate perspective of others?

_____

_____

You also *saw* yourself. Note how you saw yourself today when looking through each set of lenses.

_____

_____

_____

_____

Can you see others through the eyes of the Spirit if you are not seeing yourself through the eyes of the Spirit— while looking at yourself through the eyes of the law or flesh? What is your experience?

_____

_____

_____

_____

_____

When looking through the eyes of the Spirit, who is still outside, alien, other, apart, beyond being for, and for wanting the best?

_____

_____

_____

Many people fear that too much compassion will lead to overlooking standards, turning a blind eye to sin and just being vanilla. What is your experience? When wearing the glasses of the Spirit, do you find yourself being wishy-washy, syrupy and soft on sin? If not, how do you react?

_____

_____

_____

_____

_____

_____

_____

_____

_____

_____

_____

_____

_____

Week 5 / Day 5 / Morning

What glasses do you find yourself wearing right now? In which mode do you find yourself?

_____

_____

_____

_____

If not the mode of Spirit, what might help you resettle into that territory?

_____

_____

_____

_____

If you aren't sure, you might try this "leap of faith" from your upper, rational brain down into your emotional brain:

Since the way of the Spirit is a receiving mode, not an achieving mode, take a position that represents openness for you, a readiness to receive.

In Matthew 28:20, Jesus says he will be with His disciples always. So imagine Jesus with you. You may picture him or simply sense His presence. Perceive His compassion, His grace, His glory, His welcome, His reassurance. Let it reach not just your rational brain, but your emotional self, as well.

Hear him say things to you that he has said to others. "I see you. I am with you. I am for you, not against you. I don't condemn you. I forgive you. Receive my spirit. I will complete the work I began in you. No one can snatch you out of my hand. My peace I give you. Don't be afraid. I know the number of hairs on your head. You are mine." Imagine him touching you as he did the leper, embracing you as he described the father doing with his wayward son, or even picking you up and blessing you, as he did the little children.

Let His mercy pour down on you like rain. Soak it in. Drink it in. Sit in His peace.

When you are ready, take this experience with you into your day.

As you go through your day, saturated in the warm light of Christ and feeling whole, notice how you end up experiencing those you meet, what you end up feeling from this perspective when in their presence. Notice whether you experience being seen, accepted, wanted, welcomed, warmed, excited, happy, inspired, or possibly unseen,

unwanted, dismissed, cold, judged, deflated or burdened. The idea simply is to notice your internal reaction to the various people you meet and what happens inside of you.

List some of the people you encountered today, how you experienced them and what you felt in their presence: encouraged, discouraged, wanted, overlooked, etc.

_____
_____
_____
_____
_____
_____
_____
_____
_____
_____

Of those you listed, star two or three whose presence did the most good for your soul.

In what mode do you think those you just starred were operating—flesh, law or Spirit?

_____
_____
_____
_____
_____
_____
_____

If you sat in the presence of Jesus this morning, how would you describe your experience with him?

_____

_____

_____

_____

_____

_____

_____

_____

Which of the experiences of people you met today would you most want to give to others?

_____

_____

_____

_____

If those you encountered today responded to these same questions about their experience with you, what might they say?

_____

_____

_____

_____

_____

_____

_____

As you considered the last question, did you find yourself being compassionate, kind and encouraging to yourself—operating in a grace-filled mode? Or were you more negative, harsh and critical—in a law-filled mode?

_____

_____

_____

_____

_____

_____

_____

_____

Look over this week's journal. What strikes you? What did you find helpful? What might be worthwhile to convey to your group?

_____

_____

_____

_____

_____

_____

_____

_____

_____

_____

_____

>> **WEEK SIX**

WEEK SIX

If your group performed the feedback exercise in which group members indicated how they experienced one another, review the sheets you received from the perspective of the flesh, law and Spirit. How would you (or do you) react to the input when in each mode?

Spirit   **Law**   **Flesh**

_____

_____

_____

_____

_____

_____

_____

When you initially looked over your feedback sheets, which glasses did you have on, and what was it like for you?

_____

_____

_____

_____

Do you find it possible to receive feedback, both positive and negative, as potentially helpful insight, while not allowing the feedback to define your ultimate value?

_____

_____

_____

_____

In Luke 10:25-37, a Jewish scholar asked Jesus for feedback. Before reading the passage, fill in these blanks.

The title of the person who leads religious services in your denomination: _____

The title of someone who is ordained to serve in your denomination: _____

A type of person with whom your group would not associate: _____

As you read the exchange, insert the titles above for those corresponding in Jesus's story.

If a person told a similar story in your church, using the titles you inserted, what might the reaction be?

_____
_____
_____
_____

What kind of god did each of the characters in the story show the traveler?

_____
_____
_____
_____

As you encounter people today, ask yourself, "What kind of God do they experience when they encounter me?"

_____
_____
_____
_____
_____

Week 6 / Day 1 / Evening

As you paid attention to how others might experience you today and what kind of god they would meet when meeting you, how did this mental focus affect you? Did you find yourself gravitating toward the flesh, law or Spirit? Describe your experience of this exercise.

_____

_____

_____

_____

_____

_____

What kind of god did people meet through you today? What would you say?

_____

_____

_____

_____

Fill out one more feedback sheet, this time as if God had given it to you, and wanted your honest feedback on how you experience him. As with the other feedback sheets, this is not an assessment of God as he is described in the Bible or in doctrinal statements, but an honest reflection of your experience when you "meet with God." Find the feedback sheet on the next page.

FEEDBACK SHEET FOR GOD

Mark **NOT** what you are **SUPPOSED** to say about God, but simply provide your **EXPERIENCE** of God, how you tend to feel or respond when you think of him, pray to him, or sense His presence. Go with your gut reaction, your first impression, what feels real to you.

___

When I think of you God, I experience...

respect, value, a sense of being seen & known	*Never*	*Sometimes*	*50/50*	*Often*	*Always*
welcome, an embrace, acceptance	*Never*	*Sometimes*	*50/50*	*Often*	*Always*
judgment, measurement, being inspected or assessed	*Never*	*Sometimes*	*50/50*	*Often*	*Always*
invigoration, encouragement, energy, inspiration	*Never*	*Sometimes*	*50/50*	*Often*	*Always*
restriction, control, pressure to conform	*Never*	*Sometimes*	*50/50*	*Often*	*Always*
being enjoyed, delighted in, cherished, treasured	*Never*	*Sometimes*	*50/50*	*Often*	*Always*

tenderness, kindness, generosity, forgiveness	Never	Sometimes	50/50	Often	Always
rejection, exclusion censure, disdain	Never	Sometimes	50/50	Often	Always
hope, possibility, grace	Never	Sometimes	50/50	Often	Always
wanting to know and love God more	Never	Sometimes	50/50	Often	Always

If your group did the feedback exercise, compare the responses you just circled about how you experience God to the responses on the feedback sheets regarding other people's experience of you. Do you observe similarities? Differences? What do you notice?

_____

_____

_____

_____

_____

_____

_____

_____

Review what you marked on your feedback sheet for God, and as you do, consider how God might react to what you marked. What might he say or feel about how you experience him?

_____
_____
_____
_____
_____
_____
_____
_____
_____
_____
_____
_____
_____
_____
_____
_____
_____
_____
_____

Would you be willing to go ahead and ask him and wait for any response?

The Johari Window suggests that everyone has blind spots, and one way to increase insight and lessen blindness is to open oneself up to feedback.

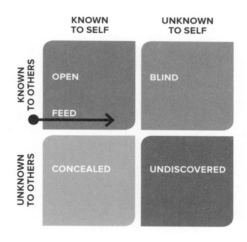

How valuable have you found others' feedback to be in your development as a person? See if you can illustrate your answer with a story.

_____

_____

_____

_____

_____

_____

_____

Have there been times when you received feedback that ended up being destructive or misled you? If so, can you describe it?

_____

_____

_____

_____

How do you discern between feedback worth considering and feedback that should be dismissed? What are some of the criteria?

_____

_____

_____

_____

_____

What would you say is the difference between feedback that assesses a person ("You are...") and feedback that conveys experiential reaction—feedback that begins, "You are..." and feedback that begins, "My experience of you is..."?

_____

_____

_____

_____

How open would you say you are to feedback when in the flesh, law and Spirit?

Spirit   **Law**   **Flesh**

_____

_____

_____

_____

_____

_____

What do you see in these passages about the worth of human feedback?

- **Proverbs 12:15**

_____

_____

- **Proverbs 27:6**

_____

_____

- **1 Corinthians 4:3**

_____

_____

- **Galatians 2**

_____

_____

Consider today whether it would be wise for you at this point to use the feedback sheet on the next page to seek feedback from others on how they experience you (and the God you represent). What motivates you to do so or not do so? Does your decision arise from the flesh, law or Spirit?

Consider from whom you might seek feedback. Would it be from friends and family, or possibly include people with whom you disagree or have been in conflict? Would the list include only Christians or perhaps those outside your faith? You might look back to Week 1, Days 3-4 where you first considered this idea.

If you desire confidential replies to enhance honesty, one way is to designate a friend to whom the responses are sent. Your friend can then arrange the feedback in a way that conceals the sources.

Weigh this decision today, in a free and open way. You even may want to seek some feedback from a trusted friend about the idea of seeking feedback in this broader fashion.

FEEDBACK SHEET FOR_____

I am taking part in a study in which I am to seek feedback about how others experience me. Would you be willing to provide me your feedback? Your responses will be confidential, as only circles are required, and your sheet will be mixed in with others. If you are willing to help me in this way, please be completely honest. You are asked NOT TO ASSESS ME, but simply to provide your EXPERIENCE OF ME—how you tend to feel or respond in my presence. Thank for considering this request to provide me with the gift of feedback.

When I am around _____ **I experience...**

respect, value, a sense of being seen & known	*Never*	*Sometimes*	*50/50*	*Often*	*Always*
welcome, an embrace, acceptance	*Never*	*Sometimes*	*50/50*	*Often*	*Always*
judgment, measurement, being inspected or assessed	*Never*	*Sometimes*	*50/50*	*Often*	*Always*
invigoration, encouragement, energy, inspiration	*Never*	*Sometimes*	*50/50*	*Often*	*Always*
restriction, control, pressure to conform	*Never*	*Sometimes*	*50/50*	*Often*	*Always*

>>CONTINUE ON NEXT PAGE

being enjoyed, delighted in, cherished, treasured	*Never*	*Sometimes*	*50/50*	*Often*	*Always*
tenderness, kindness, generosity, forgiveness	*Never*	*Sometimes*	*50/50*	*Often*	*Always*
rejection, exclusion censure, disdain	*Never*	*Sometimes*	*50/50*	*Often*	*Always*
hope, possibility, grace	*Never*	*Sometimes*	*50/50*	*Often*	*Always*
wanting to know and love God more	*Never*	*Sometimes*	*50/50*	*Often*	*Always*

As you considered seeking feedback from a wider circle of family, friends and possibly foes, what thoughts or impressions came to you?

_____

_____

_____

_____

_____

_____

How can you discern whether your conclusion arises more from a flesh, law or Spirit mode?

_____

_____

_____

_____

_____

_____

If you choose to seek further feedback, it's suggested you take action this evening by sending an explanatory email to others. People usually act more quickly when given an imminent deadline, so you might request that the feedback be returned to your contact person within three days. Explain you are asking only for five minutes to fill out the feedback and would prefer an initial, gut response, with no agonizing, fretting or hesitation.

If you choose not to seek further feedback, notice whether or not you can be at peace with this choice. If you feel some guilt or self-doubt, recognize the source, whether flesh, law or Spirit.

"Then the Lord passed in front of [Moses] and proclaimed: Yahweh - Yahweh is a compassionate and gracious God, slow to anger and rich in faithful love and truth." Exodus 34:6 HCSB

As we move toward the conclusion of this study, consider how you have been affected by using the diagram on the next page.

The inner circle represents the people who tend to receive your warmth, compassion, understanding, grace and positive concern as **your first response**. You lead with compassion. You may experience other sensations such as frustration, fear or anger, but the expression of merciful love tends to override other sensations and flow out first. Think of a loving mother's reaction to her newborn. She may be tired and frustrated at 3 a.m., but expresses soothing tenderness to the crying infant.

The outer circle represents those who tend to receive your compassion eventually, but not typically as a first response. Think of that same child as a teenager who walks in two hours after curfew at 3 a.m. A mother's anger and frustration may come out first, and the concern or understanding the next day.

Those who get compassion **eventually**

Those who get compassion **immediately**

Compassion is your **leading expression**

Those **outside** your circle of compassion

Compassion is your **later expression**

Beyond both circles lies those who never receive your compassion **as they are**. The "friend" who kept the teenager out until 3 a.m. and has also gotten him addicted to alcohol, marijuana and meth may receive zero compassion from the teen's mother. She would say, "This 'friend' is a problem who needs to get out of my son's life." However, if that "friend" fessed up and tried to turn his life around, the mother might allow him probational status in her outer circle of compassion.

Today, keep in mind these three circles. As you encounter others, ask yourself, "Does this person receive compassion as my lead offering, or does he receive compassion only later—or possibly not at all? Also notice if your reaction is different from when you first began "God for the Rest of Us."

Week 6 / Day 3 / Evening

Jot names or initials of some of those who tend to occupy each area for you. If they have "moved" in any way during this study, indicate where they began and where they are at this juncture.

_____

_____

_____

_____

_____

_____

_____

_____

If you have not done so already, put your initials on the diagram to reflect how you approached yourself today—whether with immediate compassion, eventual compassion or no compassion. Also indicate if the location has changed during the course of these weeks.

_____

_____

_____

Should a Christ follower always lead with compassion? How would you answer?

_____

_____

_____

_____

_____

_____

_____

Does leading with compassion mean a person is soft, doesn't speak the hard truth and is condoning the wrongs of those who receive his compassion? If the term "Christ follower" is not just a designation but an actual description, then such people would imitate the example of Jesus. As we have seen in this journal, Jesus often is described as being full of compassion and leading with compassion. What do you see as His leading expression, and toward whom, in these two passages? Also note the reason for this disposition.

• **Mark 2:23-3:6**

_____

_____

_____

_____

• **Matthew 23:13-33**

_____

_____

_____

_____

Based on your understanding of Jesus, what sorts of people would he put in each area?

_____

_____

_____

_____

_____

_____

_____

_____

Where do you believe Jesus would put you on His diagram? After writing your name, take a few minutes to meditate on the diagram, sensing how it strikes you.

Look back at the yesterday's diagrams. What determines whether a person receives compassion from you first, later or not at all?

_____

_____

_____

_____

As far as you can see, what determines whether a person receives compassion from Jesus first, later, or not at all?

_____

_____

_____

What is your reaction to these two statements?

• *A sign of being in the law is: we give people what we think they most deserve.*

• *A sign of being in the Spirit is: we give people what we perceive they need most.*

_____

_____

_____

_____

_____

In looking back at your diagram, which is closer to how you decide who gets compassion—by what they deserve or what they need?

_____

_____

_____

Today notice which of these two paths your automatic brain takes. Do you think first about what the other probably deserves or what the other likely needs?

What is your reaction to today's exercise? What did you notice?

_____

_____

_____

_____

What is the effect on you when you are in the "give what they deserve" mode, and when you are in the "give what they need" mode?

_____

_____

_____

_____

What would you say you deserved most from others today?

_____

_____

_____

_____

What would you say you needed most from others today?

_____

_____

_____

_____

Which of the two did you receive today, and from whom?

_____

_____

_____

_____

What did you give yourself, what you think you deserved or what you perceived you really needed?

_____

_____

_____

_____

What strikes you from Luke 6:27-38?

_____
_____
_____
_____

What is the basis for treating others in the way
described in this passage?

_____
_____
_____
_____

As you pray tonight, will you ask your heavenly Father
for what you deserve or what you need?

_____
_____
_____
_____

Which do you believe he wants you to request, what
you deserve or what you need?

_____
_____
_____
_____
_____
_____

*"The Spirit of the Lord is on me, because he has anointed me to proclaim good news to the poor. He has sent me to proclaim freedom for the prisoners and **recovery of sight for the blind,** to set the oppressed free, to proclaim the year of the Lord's favor."*
Luke 4:18-19

You have reached the last day of this journal. Today reflect on how this study has affected you, using our old friend, the Johari Window.

• To what have you been formerly blind or had yet to discover, but now are aware?
• What were you previously concealing from others that you now are making more open?

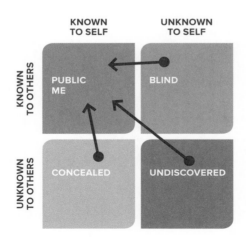

Think about this question as you walk through your day, encountering and relating to others. You may want to take some time to flip back through your journal to enhance your reflection, as well.

Also, if you requested feedback from others, retrieve it from your designated contact person.

Week 6 / Day 5 / Evening

How has this study affected you? Use the Johari Window if you find it helpful.

_____

_____

_____

_____

_____

_____

_____

_____

_____

_____

_____

_____

_____

_____

_____

Do you foresee yourself holding onto—or even building onto—these insights and changes, or do you expect what you gained to slowly fade as your emotional brain settles back into its old place? What do you anticipate and why?

_____

_____

_____

_____

_____

_____

_____

_____

_____

_____

_____

_____

_____

_____

_____

_____

_____

_____

_____

_____

_____

_____

EVER WIDENING CIRCLES

Before your next group session, review the postscript to this study, "Ever Widening Circles."

Ever Widening Circles:
Extending "God for the Rest of Us"
to the Outer Edges of Your World

You have three brains.

That is how this journal began, with a delineation between your lower brain, your middle or emotional brain and your upper, rational brain.
Since the emotional mid-brain can learn but not think, and its ruts are deep, and as it takes time for this automatic part of your neuro-anatomy to be retrained, your upper brain can intellectually "know" something in a new way, but your mid-brain may not be on board yet. It doesn't "believe."

It's unlikely that any significant realizations you have

had will take root in a six-week time frame. These seeds can quickly be choked out by the worries and busyness of life.

So how does one make recent, raw realizations into recurring, reflexive reactions?

This postscript suggests one method with which to experiment over the next six weeks. It continues with a pattern of morning and evening reflections, and takes about 10 minutes a day.

Each morning look ahead in your day. Choose one event or encounter upon which to focus. You might choose one involving a person on the outer fringes of your circles of compassion; someone whom you are struggling to see with grace-filled eyes. Or you may choose an ordinary, everyday event.

Next, enter a prayerful, reflective mindset. Ask the Spirit to show you how you would approach this encounter if wearing the glasses of the flesh—if it were all about you getting what you want. How would that encounter likely go? See it play out in your mind. Then take a snapshot of that encounter, as if a photographer caught the essence of the moment. Hold this mental snapshot in your hand, and imagine flicking on a lighter and setting fire to the photo. Watch it disintegrate.

Next ask the Spirit how you would approach this encounter if looking through the lens of the law, trying to justify yourself, do the right thing and follow the rules. Play that scenario out. Take a snapshot capturing 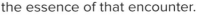 the essence of that encounter. Then burn this photo, as well. Watch its edges curl and the whole thing go up in smoke.

Now imagine yourself being filled with the Spirit, full of light, love and joy. See Jesus full of extravagant, irrational, unrestrained compassion welcoming you, smiling at you, speaking to you words of absolute acceptance, complete forgiveness and unending tenderness. Let all fear, worry and the need to prove yourself drain away. Let yourself smile as you re-receive grace.

While in this state, imagine yourself entering your chosen encounter. Play out what happens on the screen of your mind. Watch yourself living in the Spirit and walking in the Spirit. Turn the essence of this encounter into a photograph. Put this photo in a beautiful frame, and set the picture on a shelf in your mind. It has a permanent place. This is the real you. Step back and look at it, with Jesus beside you.

What you have just done is transform your prayer into an actual preparation for life. When you enter that encounter today, consciously take the picture down off the shelf, and carry it with you as a reminder of your preparation.

Each evening, take that day's framed photograph down off the shelf of your mind. Hold it up beside a photo of how the encounter actually took place. How are they alike? How are they different? What did you learn? What does Jesus say to you?

At the end of each week, draw the two circles of compassion from Week 6. Jot the names in the appropriate location of those you "photographed" this week Include your name, as well. Notice if your circles have gotten any "wider," so to speak.

Close your week by turning Ephesians 3:14-21 into your own prayer.

Small groups are encouraged to do *Ever Widening Circles* together, allowing whomever wishes a couple of minutes to share at the group gatherings. If you group is not doing *Ever Widening Circles* together, it would enhance your efforts to invite a friend to experiment with you, and converse over what you experience.

If you or your group found this study meaningful, and would like to undertake another City on a Hill study, *AHA* would be a nice compliment to what you just have completed. You can see a preview of this study at **www.CityOnAHillStudio.com**. If you have feedback for us, we would love to hear it. You may contact us at **info@cityonahillstudio.com**.